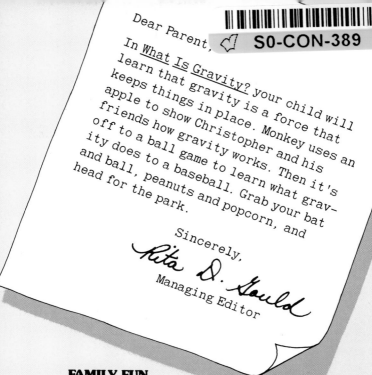

Dear Parent,

In <u>What Is Gravity?</u> your child will learn that gravity is a force that keeps things in place. Monkey uses an apple to show Christopher and his friends how gravity works. Then it's off to a ball game to learn what gravity does to a baseball. Grab your bat and ball, peanuts and popcorn, and head for the park.

Sincerely,

Rita D. Gould
Managing Editor

FAMILY FUN

- Demonstrate how gravity works. Have your child stand on a chair or bench and drop a bean bag (a heavy object) to the floor. Have your child drop the bean bag and a pencil (a light object) at the same time. Help your child understand that both hit the floor at the same time.

- Some lightweight objects catch air currents as they fall, slowing down the fall. Have your child stand on a chair and drop a bean bag and a sheet of paper at the same time. Help your child understand why the paper falls more slowly than the bean bag.

READ MORE ABOUT IT

- *Why Does It Fly?*
- *What Is a Space Shuttle?*
- *What Is a Wave?*

This book is
a presentation of Newfield Publications, Inc.
Newfield Publications offers book clubs for children from
preschool through high school. For further information write to:
Newfield Publications, Inc.,
4343 Equity Drive, Columbus, Ohio 43228.

This edition is published
by arrangement with Checkerboard Press, Inc.
Newfield Publications and design are federally registered
trademarks of Newfield Publications, Inc.

1995 edition

What Is Gravity?

A **Just Ask**™ Book

Hi, my name is Christopher!

by Chris Arvetis
and Carole Palmer

illustrated by
Vernon McKissack

NEWFIELD
PUBLICATIONS
SHELTON, CONNECTICUT

When I jump off this rock,
I fall to the ground.
You try it, too.

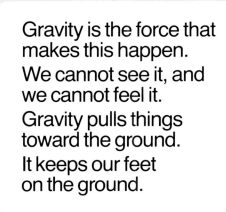

Gravity is the force that makes this happen.
We cannot see it, and we cannot feel it.
Gravity pulls things toward the ground.
It keeps our feet on the ground.

Just imagine if we lived in a place where there was no gravity.
Look at these pictures.
They show what it would be like.
See our friends floating in the air.

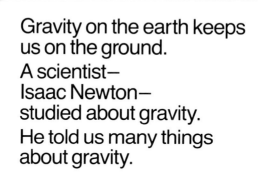

Gravity on the earth keeps
us on the ground.
A scientist—
Isaac Newton—
studied about gravity.
He told us many things
about gravity.

We can see this if we look at a ball game.
The ball keeps on moving as long as the players are hitting it back and forth.

Once the ball stops, someone or something has to make it move.

Or gravity will hold the ball right where it is.

Gravity holds you on the ground and keeps things in place around you.
It is a part of our world on earth.